W9-DEZ-268

COUNTRY PROFILES

NEPAL

BY ALICIA Z. KLEPEIS

BELLWETHER MEDIA • MINNEAPOLIS, MN

BLASTOFF!
DISCOVERY

Blastoff! Discovery launches a new mission: reading to learn. Filled with facts and features, each book offers you an exciting new world to explore!

BLASTOFF! UNIVERSE

BLASTOFF! Beginners — GRADE K

BLASTOFF! READERS — GRADES 1-3

BLASTOFF! DISCOVERY — GRADE 4

This edition first published in 2021 by Bellwether Media, Inc.

No part of this publication may be reproduced in whole or in part without written permission of the publisher.
For information regarding permission, write to Bellwether Media, Inc.,
Attention: Permissions Department,
6012 Blue Circle Drive, Minnetonka, MN 55343.

Library of Congress Cataloging-in-Publication Data

Names: Klepeis, Alicia, 1971- author.
Title: Nepal / by Alicia Z. Klepeis.
Description: Minneapolis, MN : Bellwether Media, 2021. |
    Series: Blastoff! Discovery: Country Profiles | Includes
    bibliographical references and index.
Audience: Ages 7-13 | Audience: Grades 4-6 | Summary: "Engaging
images accompany information about Nepal. The combination of
high-interest subject matter and narrative text is intended for students
in grades 3 through 8"– Provided by publisher.
Identifiers: LCCN 2020049049 (print) | LCCN 2020049050 (ebook)
    | ISBN 9781644874509 (library binding) | ISBN
    9781648341274 (ebook)
Subjects: LCSH: Nepal–Juvenile literature. | Nepal–Social life and
    customs–Juvenile literature.
Classification: LCC DS493.4 .K58 2021 (print) | LCC DS493.4
(ebook) | DDC 954.96–dc23
LC record available at https://lccn.loc.gov/2020049049
LC ebook record available at https://lccn.loc.gov/2020049050

Editor: Kieran Downs   Designer: Laura Sowers

Printed in the United States of America, North Mankato, MN.

TABLE OF CONTENTS

CHITWAN NATIONAL PARK   4
LOCATION   6
LANDSCAPE AND CLIMATE   8
WILDLIFE   10
PEOPLE   12
COMMUNITIES   14
CUSTOMS   16
SCHOOL AND WORK   18
PLAY   20
FOOD   22
CELEBRATIONS   24
TIMELINE   26
NEPAL FACTS   28
GLOSSARY   30
TO LEARN MORE   31
INDEX   32

CHITWAN
NATIONAL PARK

On a mild winter morning, a jeep full of **tourists** arrives at Chitwan National Park. Baby rhinos curiously watch as the tourists drive toward park headquarters. The visitors head to the Gharial Crocodile Breeding Project. They get a close-up view of these rare baby crocodiles.

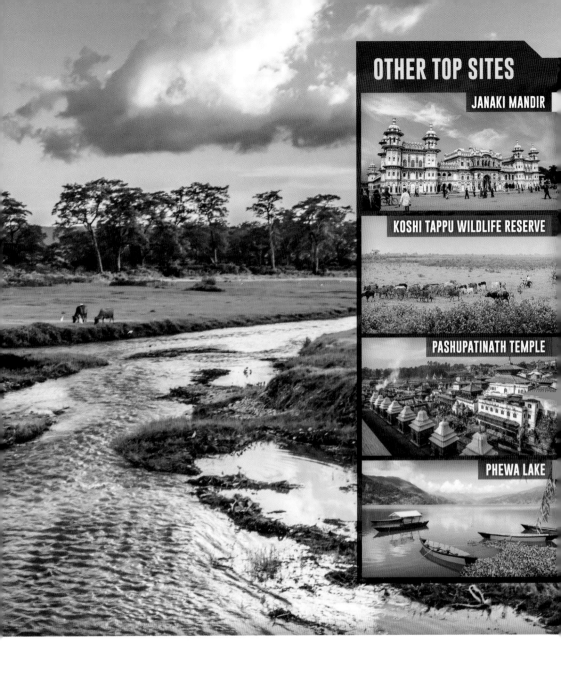

OTHER TOP SITES

JANAKI MANDIR

KOSHI TAPPU WILDLIFE RESERVE

PASHUPATINATH TEMPLE

PHEWA LAKE

The tourists take a guided wildlife tour after lunch. The call of a barking deer can be heard from a distance. Rhesus monkeys swing among the trees. Parakeets flit about as colorful kingfishers swoop down to snatch up frogs and fish. At dusk, the group watches animals along a nearby river. Welcome to Nepal!

CHINA

NEPAL

POKHARA

KATHMANDU

LALITPUR

INDIA

BIRATNAGAR

Nepal is located in southern Asia. The nation covers 56,827 square miles (147,181 square kilometers). It is about the same size as the state of Iowa. Kathmandu is the capital city. It lies in a high valley in central Nepal.

Nepal is a **landlocked** country. No oceans touch its borders. The Chinese region of Tibet borders Nepal to the north. India is Nepal's neighbor on the east, south, and west.

Nepal's land varies in **elevation**. In the south is the Tarai. This lowland area is flat with **fertile** soil. The hill region stretches across central Nepal. It has wide valleys and hills rising into the Mahābhārat Range of northern Nepal. This range is also called the Lower Himalayas. The High Himalayas feature some of the world's tallest mountains, including Mount Everest. Many of the country's rivers, such as the Kosi and Karnali, begin there as well.

KARNALI RIVER
MOUNT EVEREST
KOSI RIVER

= HIGH HIMALAYAS
= TARAI

TARAI

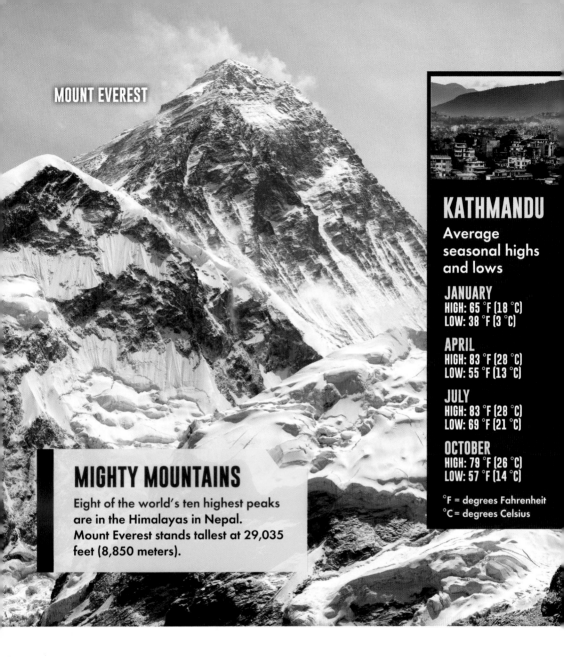

MOUNT EVEREST

KATHMANDU

Average seasonal highs and lows

JANUARY
HIGH: 65 °F (18 °C)
LOW: 38 °F (3 °C)

APRIL
HIGH: 83 °F (28 °C)
LOW: 55 °F (13 °C)

JULY
HIGH: 83 °F (28 °C)
LOW: 69 °F (21 °C)

OCTOBER
HIGH: 79 °F (26 °C)
LOW: 57 °F (14 °C)

°F = degrees Fahrenheit
°C = degrees Celsius

MIGHTY MOUNTAINS

Eight of the world's ten highest peaks are in the Himalayas in Nepal. Mount Everest stands tallest at 29,035 feet (8,850 meters).

Southern Nepal is hot and humid. **Monsoons** bring heavy rains between June and September. The climate gets cooler at higher elevations. Northern Nepal has an **alpine** climate. Summers are cool and winters are cold.

WILDLIFE

Nepal is home to a wide variety of wildlife. In the jungles of the Tarai, sloth bears dig for ants and pluck mangoes from trees. Chital deer graze on grasses and mushrooms while looking out for leopards and Bengal tigers. King cobras hide in the swamps.

Hundreds of bird species live in Nepal. Blue-throated barbets, rose-ringed parakeets, and common cuckoos thrill birdwatchers with their brilliant colors. The Himalayas are home to yaks and tahr. They easily climb the rough **terrain** of the high mountains. Snow leopards often prey on blue sheep.

BENGAL TIGER

BLUE-THROATED BARBET

HIMALAYAN TAHR

KING COBRA

SNOW LEOPARD

SLOTH BEAR

SLOTH BEAR

Life Span: up to 25 years
Red List Status: vulnerable

sloth bear range =

LEAST CONCERN	NEAR THREATENED	VULNERABLE	ENDANGERED	CRITICALLY ENDANGERED	EXTINCT IN THE WILD	EXTINCT

More than 30 million people call Nepal home. People from Nepal are called Nepalis. They belong to many different **ethnic** groups. The two biggest groups are the Brahman-Hill and the Chhettri people. Other groups include the Tharu, Tamang, Magar, and Newar. People from India and Tibet also live in Nepal.

More than 8 out of 10 Nepalis are Hindus. The second-most followed religion is Buddhism. Less than half of the population speaks Nepali, the nation's official language. People speak many other languages such as Maithali and Bhojpuri. English is growing among **urban** residents and business people.

FAMOUS FACE

Name: Sandeep Lamichhane
Birthday: August 2, 2000
Hometown: Aruchaur, Syangja, Nepal
Famous for: Member of Nepal's national cricket team and the first Nepali cricketer to play in the Indian Premier League

SPEAK NEPALI

Nepali uses script instead of letters. However, Nepali words can be written with the English alphabet so you can read them.

ENGLISH	NEPALI	HOW TO SAY IT
hello	namaste	nah-MAH-stay
goodbye	namaste	nah-MAH-stay
please	kripaya	kree-PIE-yah
thank you	dhanyabad	DHAN-nai-bad
yes	ho	HOE
no	hoina	hoe-ee-NAH

LALITPUR

About four out of five Nepalis live in **rural** areas. Houses in the countryside are made of mud, bamboo, or stone. The houses usually do not have running water but often have electricity. People commonly travel on foot or by bicycle. Animals such as yaks are often used for transportation, too.

JEWEL IN THE HIMALAYA

Nepal's second-largest city, Pokhara, is nicknamed the "Jewel in the Himalaya." Among its many treasures are Phewa Lake, Devi's Falls, and the World Peace Pagoda.

WORLD PEACE
PAGODA

KATHMANDU

More and more people in Nepal are moving to urban areas. The nation's largest city is Kathmandu. Over 1 million people live there. City dwellers often live in single-family homes or apartments. People in Nepali cities get around by bus, taxi, or motorcycle.

NAMASTE
GREETING

Greetings in Nepal often vary by language. One common greeting is *namaste*. Nepalis hold their palms together upright in front of their chests or chins. Another common greeting is asking *khana khanu bhayo?* This means "have you eaten your rice already?"

Dance and music are well-loved pastimes among Nepalis. Ethnic groups often have their own dances. Some dances tell stories. Others, such as Chandi Naach, celebrate religious beliefs. **Traditional** Nepali music often uses wooden flutes and drums. A very popular instrument is the four-stringed *sarangi*. It is often played while people dance and sing.

SARANGI

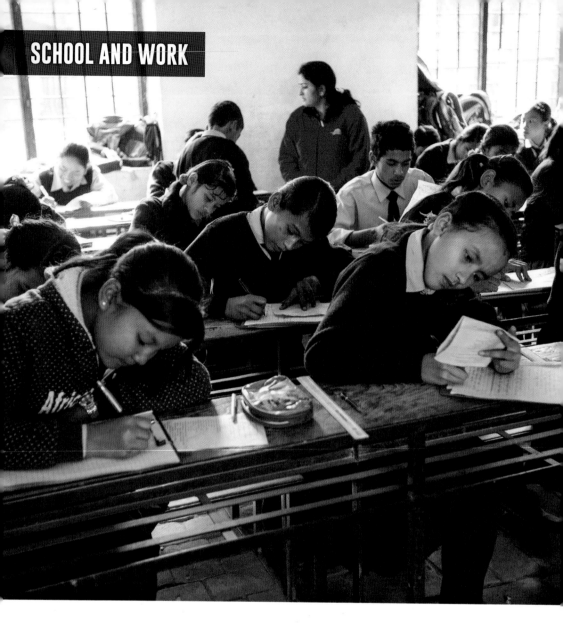

Children in Nepal typically begin primary school at age 6. Primary school lasts for five years. Students are required to attend school through grade 8. They study Nepali, math, science, and other subjects. Some students continue their secondary education though grade 12. Most college students in Nepal attend Tribhuvan University.

Nearly 7 out of 10 Nepalis work in agriculture. Most grow food for their families to eat. Farmers also grow cash crops including rice, wheat, potatoes, sugarcane, **jute**, and corn. Tourism brings in a lot of money for the nation. Nepali workers also **manufacture** products including clothing and carpets.

RICE FARMER

MOUNTAINS AND MONEY

Tourists climbing Mount Everest bring in a lot of money for Nepal. Each person must pay $11,000 dollars for a permit to climb.

In 2017, Nepal's government made volleyball the national sport. Kids often play it at school. Villages across Nepal have outdoor volleyball courts. Other popular sports include soccer, badminton, and cricket. *Dandi biyo* is a traditional sport in Nepal. Players try to use a longer stick to hit a shorter one as far as they can.

DANDI BIYO

Many Nepalis have little free time because of their work demands. However, Nepalis often enjoy watching television for fun. Urban Nepalis can also see movies in theaters. Swimming is another popular activity across Nepal. It is unusual for people to go on family vacations.

DIWALI DIYAS

Diwali, also known as *Tihar* in Nepal, is the Hindu festival of lights. Make your own clay lamp known as a **diya**!

What You Need:
- air-dry clay
- acrylic paint or permanent markers (optional)
- LED candle
- pencil or **toothpick**

Instructions:
1. Look online or in a **book** at some images of diyas.
2. Take a piece of clay **that is between the size of a golf ball and a baseball. Roll it into a ball.**
3. Mold the clay into a bowl shape. Make sure the lamp is not too deep or you will not see the candlelight well. Flatten the bottom of the bowl so the diya can rest flat on a table.
4. Use a toothpick or pencil to make designs or patterns in the clay.
5. Let the clay air dry completely. If desired, paint or color the dried lamp.
6. Place your LED candle inside the finished diya. Enjoy!

RELIGION AND MEAT

Hindus do not eat beef because cows are sacred in their religion. It is against the Muslim faith to eat pork. Some Buddhists in Nepal do not eat any meat.

MOMOS

People in Nepal often eat *dal bhat*, a lentil soup served with rice. Curried vegetables, known as *tarakari*, are often served alongside it. Another popular food is *momos*. These steamed dumplings can be filled with either vegetables or meat. Fish curry is a common dish in the Tarai region.

Yak cheese called *chhurpi* is enjoyed in the Himalayas. A popular snack is *sel roti*, a sweet fried doughnut made of rice flour. Nepalis also snack on dried fruit such as mango and apricots. *Chaku* is a very sweet candy made from molasses, milk, and butter.

CHHURPI

SEL ROTI

NEPALI DAL

Have an adult help you make this recipe!

Ingredients:
2 tablespoons vegetable oil
1 onion, chopped
2 cloves garlic, minced
1 1/2 teaspoons grated fresh ginger
1 teaspoon coriander
1/2 teaspoon turmeric
1/2 teaspoon chili powder
1 cup red lentils, rinsed
3 cups water
3/4 teaspoon salt
2 tablespoons cilantro

Steps:
1. Pour the oil into a deep pan and warm over medium-heat. Add the onion to the pan and cook for about 5 to 7 minutes until softened.

2. Turn the heat to low. Add the garlic, ginger, coriander, turmeric, and chili powder. Stir and cook for 3 minutes longer.

3. Add the lentils to the pan. Stir for 2 to 3 minutes to coat them in the spice-onion mixture.

4. Add the water to the pan and bring to a boil. Add the salt. Once boiling, turn the heat down to medium-low. Simmer for 15 to 18 minutes.

5. Stir in the cilantro. Take the pan off the heat, serve with rice, and enjoy!

CELEBRATIONS

The Nepali New Year takes place in April. People will often throw parties with food to celebrate. *Buddha Jayanti* celebrates Buddha's birth in April or May. Families dress in all white and meet to pray and **meditate**. September 20 is Constitution Day across Nepal. Parades are part of the festivities.

Dashain, the country's biggest holiday, occurs in September or October. It celebrates the victory of good over evil. Nepalis exchange gifts and have feasts during this 15-day-long holiday. They also worship Durga, the Hindu goddess of victory. Nepalis celebrate their **culture** and country all year long!

DASHAIN

A COLORFUL CELEBRATION

Holi is a Hindu festival marking the start of spring. A unique part of the celebration includes people throwing colored powders on each other. Each color has its own special meaning.

HOLI

TIMELINE

1768
A Gurkha ruler named Prithvi Narayan Shah conquers Kathmandu and sets up framework for a unified kingdom

7TH OR 8TH CENTURY BCE
The Hindu Kiratis arrive in what is now Nepal and become the first rulers of the Kathmandu Valley

AROUND 563 BCE
Prince Siddhartha Gautama, the founder of Buddhism, is born in Lumbini

1816
Nepal's current borders are set after the Anglo-Nepalese War

1923
Great Britain signs a treaty that recognizes Nepal as an independent country ruled by a monarch

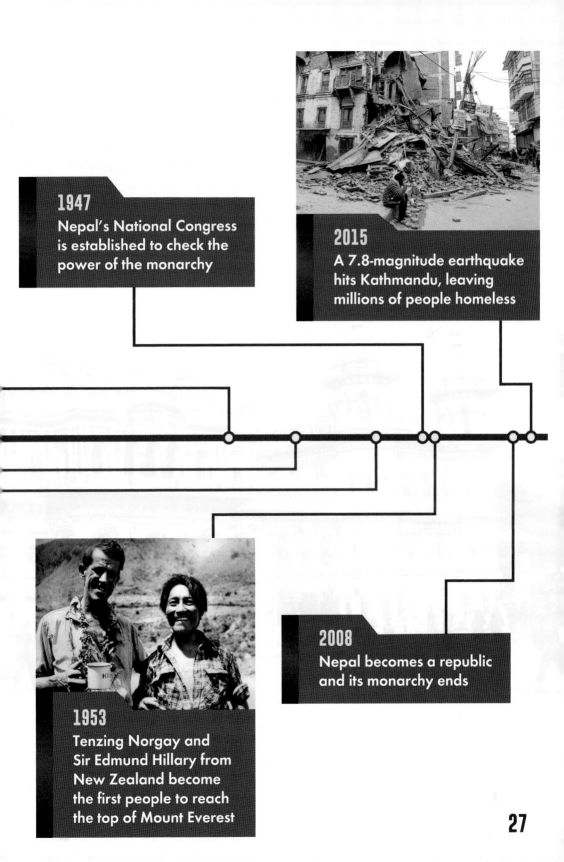

1947
Nepal's National Congress is established to check the power of the monarchy

2015
A 7.8-magnitude earthquake hits Kathmandu, leaving millions of people homeless

2008
Nepal becomes a republic and its monarchy ends

1953
Tenzing Norgay and Sir Edmund Hillary from New Zealand become the first people to reach the top of Mount Everest

NEPAL FACTS

Official Name: Federal Democratic Republic of Nepal

Flag of Nepal: Nepal's flag is the only one in the world that is not a rectangle. Two overlapping triangles, which represent Hinduism and Buddhism, form its shape. Both are red with a blue border. Blue stands for peace and harmony, while red stands for victory and bravery. The upper triangle features a white moon with eight rays coming out. The lower triangle contains a white sun. These symbols are meant to show hope that the nation will last as long as the moon and sun.

Area: 56,827 square miles
(147,181 square kilometers)

Capital City: Kathmandu

Important Cities: Pokhara, Lalitpur, Biratnagar

Population:
30,327,877 (2020 est.)

WHERE PEOPLE LIVE

COUNTRYSIDE
79.4%

CITY
20.6%

MANUFACTURING
12%

JOBS

SERVICES
19%

FARMING
69%

Main Exports:

fabrics

spices

carpets

flavored water

plastic products

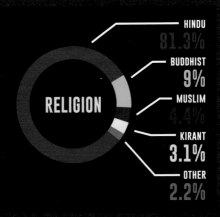

National Holiday:
Constitution Day (September 20)

Main Language:
Nepali (official)

Form of Government:
federal parliamentary republic

Title for Country Leaders:
president (head of state),
prime minister (head of government)

HINDU
81.3%

BUDDHIST
9%

MUSLIM
4.4%

RELIGION

KIRANT
3.1%

OTHER
2.2%

Unit of Money:
Nepalese rupee

GLOSSARY

alpine—relating to the cold climate found in the mountains

culture—the beliefs, arts, and ways of life in a place or society

elevation—the height above sea level

ethnic—related to a group of people who share customs and an identity

fertile—able to support growth

jute—a fiber from two types of Asian plants which is often used to make twine and sacks

landlocked—enclosed or almost completely enclosed by land

manufacture—to make products, often with machines

meditate—to quietly think or reflect for religious purposes or relaxation

monsoons—winds that shift direction each season; monsoons bring heavy rain.

rural—related to the countryside

terrain—the surface features of an area of land

tourists—people who travel to visit another place

traditional—related to customs, ideas, or beliefs handed down from one generation to the next

urban—related to cities and city life

TO LEARN MORE

AT THE LIBRARY

Bailey, Diane. *My Teenage Life in Nepal*. Broomall, Penn.: Mason Crest Publishers, 2018.

Mattern, Joanne. *Nepal*. New York, N.Y.: Cavendish Square Publishing, 2018.

Oachs, Emily Rose. *India*. Minneapolis, Minn.: Bellwether Media, 2018.

ON THE WEB

FACTSURFER

Factsurfer.com gives you a safe, fun way to find more information.

1. Go to www.factsurfer.com.

2. Enter "Nepal" into the search box and click Q.

3. Select your book cover to see a list of related content.

INDEX

activities, 17, 21
Buddha Jayanti, 24
capital (see Kathmandu)
celebrations, 24-25
Chitwan National Park, 4-5
climate, 9
communities, 14-15, 20
Constitution Day, 24
customs, 16-17
Dashain, 24
Diwali diyas (activity), 21
education, 18
fast facts, 28-29
food, 19, 22-23
Himalayas, 8, 9, 10, 14, 23
Holi, 25
housing, 14, 15
Kathmandu, 6, 7, 9, 15
Lalitpur, 6, 13
Lamichhane, Sandeep, 13
landmarks, 4, 5, 14
landscape, 8-9, 10, 19
language, 13, 16, 18
location, 6-7
Mount Everest, 8, 9, 19

music, 17
Nepali New Year, 24
people, 12-13, 17
Pokhara, 6, 14
recipe, 23
religion, 13, 17, 22, 24, 25
size, 7
sports, 20
timeline, 26-27
transportation, 14, 15
wildlife, 4, 5, 10-11
work, 19, 21